THE PRAYING ATHLETE™
QUOTE BOOK

VOL 3

GROWTH & PREPARATION
FOR THE FUTURE

Published by The Core Media Group, Inc., P.O. Box 2037, Indian Trail, NC 28079.

Cover & Interior Design: Ashlyn Helms

Printed in the United States of America.

VOL 3 GROWTH & PREP. FOR THE FUTURE

**Make the most of your time now.
We all will be replaced at
some point.**

"Teach us to number our days, that we
may gain a heart of wisdom."
Psalm 90:12

Getting stronger does not always mean physically, but rather mentally, emotionally, and spiritually.

"I pray that out of his glorious riches he may strengthen you with power through his Spirit in your inner being."
Ephesians 3:16

Habits are hard to develop and break. Make your good habits a thing of the present and future, and make your bad habits a thing of the past.

"If we confess our sins, he is faithful and just and will forgive us our sins and purify us from all unrighteousness."
1 John 1:9

**Never allow minor challenges to
sidetrack your mental focus,
use the minor challenges
to build the foundation of
your mental strength.**

"Consider it pure joy, my brothers and
sisters, whenever you face trials of
many kinds, because you know that the
testing of your faith produces
perseverance. Let perseverance finish
its work so that you may be mature and
complete, not lacking anything."
James 1:2-4

Doing the same things over and over again will result in a continuation of the past. If you don't want history to repeat itself, you have to adjust your game plan.

"Whatever you have learned or received or heard from me, or seen in me – put it into practice. And the God of peace will be with you."
Philippians 4:9

When you think the race is finished it is just beginning, one victory does not mean the race of life is completed. Keep pushing!

"Therefore, since we are surrounded by such a great cloud of witnesses, let us throw off everything that hinders and the sin that so easily entangles. And let us run with perseverance the race marked out for us."
Hebrews 12:1

What is the destination of your life? Draw a map and layout your plan and destination. You cannot get to where you want to go if you do not have a plan in mind. Plan ahead to arrive on time.

"In their hearts humans plan their course, but the Lord establishes their steps."
Proverbs 16:9

Those who define greatness achieve greatness. If you cannot define greatness for your life, you cannot find it. Define greatness for yourself and you will find and achieve greatness.

"You will increase my honor and comfort me once more."
Psalm 71:21

**Courage is fear wrapped in the
sweat of preparation.**

"Be watchful, stand firm in the faith,
act like men, be strong."
1 Corinthians 16:13

**Your mindset can counter
any setback.**

"Finally, brothers and sisters, whatever
is true, whatever is noble, whatever
is right, whatever is pure, whatever
is lovely, whatever is admirable – if
anything is excellent or praiseworthy –
think about such things."
Philippians 4:8

**Trophies all end up in the attic.
Enjoy your achievements, but
keep your focus on the future.**

"Being confident of this, that he who
began a good work in you will carry it
on to completion until the
day of Christ Jesus."
Philippians 1:6

Control your thoughts with a winning attitude.

"Do not conform to the pattern of this world, but be transformed by the renewing of your mind. Then you will be able to test and approve that God's will is – his good, pleasing and perfect will."
Romans 12:2

Life is 10% what happens to you and 90% how you respond to it.

"Slaves, in reverent fear of God submit
yourselves to your masters, not only to
those who are good and considerate,
but also to those who are harsh."
1 Peter 2:18

What do you need to sacrifice to achieve your goals, dreams and vision for your life?

"Therefore, I urge you, brothers and sisters, in view of God's mercy, to offer your bodies as a living sacrifice, holy and pleasing to God – this is your true and proper worship.
Romans 12:1

Who are you coaching in life? We are all coaches in our own way. Remind yourself of that fact, and it will help you have greater impact on others.

"In the same way, let your light shine before others, that they may see your good deeds and glorify your Father in heaven."
Matthew 5:16

Before you weigh in, drop off your cares and burdens into God's grace. You will see your heart will be much lighter.

"Cast all your anxiety on him because he cares for you."
1 Peter 5:7

People always say I want to be this or that, but they are never willing to make the commitment and sacrifice to attain those goals.

"Commit your way to the Lord; trust in him and he will do this."
Psalm 37:5

Many people will say you cannot do it, few will say you can.

"Jesus looked at them and said, 'With man this is impossible, but with God all things are possible.'"
Matthew 19:26

Building your own success is much more important than someone handing you success.

"And observe what the Lord your God requires: Walk in obedience to him, and keep his decrees and commands, his laws and regulations, as written in the Law of Moses. Do this so that you may prosper in all you do and wherever you go."
1 Kings 2:3

**Having a plan and implementing
a plan are totally different.
Take steps to implement your
plan today.**

"The plans of the diligent lead to profit
as surely as haste leads to poverty."
Proverbs 21:5

**Where you come from cannot
hold you back from where you
want to go, only you can.**

"There is neither Jew nor Gentile,
neither slave nor free, nor is there male
and female, for you are all
one in Christ Jesus."
Galatians 3:28

**Extraordinary moments don't
take place without extraordinary
preparation along the way.**

"Suppose one of you wants to build
a tower. Won't you first sit down
and estimate the cost to see if you have
enough money to complete it?"
Luke 14:28

Chase the money and lose the dream; chase the dream, and the money will come to you.

"For the love of money is a root of all kinds of evil. Some people, eager for money, have wandered form the faith and pierced themselves with many griefs."
1 Timothy 6:10

What is behind me is done forever and cannot be changed. I am headed before me, toward my dreams and goals.

"Brothers and sisters, I do not consider myself yet to have taken hold of it. But one thing I do: Forgetting what is behind and straining toward what is ahead, I press on toward the goal to win the prize for which God has called me heavenward in Christ Jesus."
Philippians 3:13-14

**Losses uncover your
areas of need. Embrace them.
Failure is a great teacher.**

"But he said to me, 'My grace is
sufficient for you, for my power is
made perfect in weakness.'
Therefore I will boast all the more
gladly about my weaknesses, so that
Christ's power may rest on me."
2 Corinthians 12:9

Every day, do something to take off and make your dreams happen. If you do nothing, nothing will happen. Take off today.

"Flee the evil desires of the youth and pursue righteousness, faith, love, and peace, along with those who call on the Lord out of a pure heart."
2 Timothy 2:22

**When you feel like your hopes
and dreams are fading
away just hang on!
That is a feeling not a fact!**

"Not only so, but we also glory in our
sufferings, because we know that
suffering produces perseverance;
perseverance, character; and
character, hope."
Romans 5:3-4

Never let a day pass without taking a step toward your dreams. This is the only way they become reality.

"Strengthening the disciples and encouraging them to remain true to the faith. 'We must go through many hardships to enter the kingdom of God," they said."
Acts 14:22

Breakaway from whatever it is that's keeping you from achieving your goals.

"If we confess our sins, he is faithful and just and will forgive us our sins and purify us from unrighteousness."
1 John 1:9

They say good things come to those who wait. I say good things come to those who work.

"And with you, Lord, is unfailing love; and, You reward everyone according to what they have done."
Psalm 62:12

THOUGHTS & REFLECTIONS

_____

_____

_____

_____

_____

_____

_____

_____

_____

_____

_____

_____

_____

_____

_____

_____

_____

_____

_____

_____

_____

_____

_____

_____

_____

_____

_____

_____

_____

_____

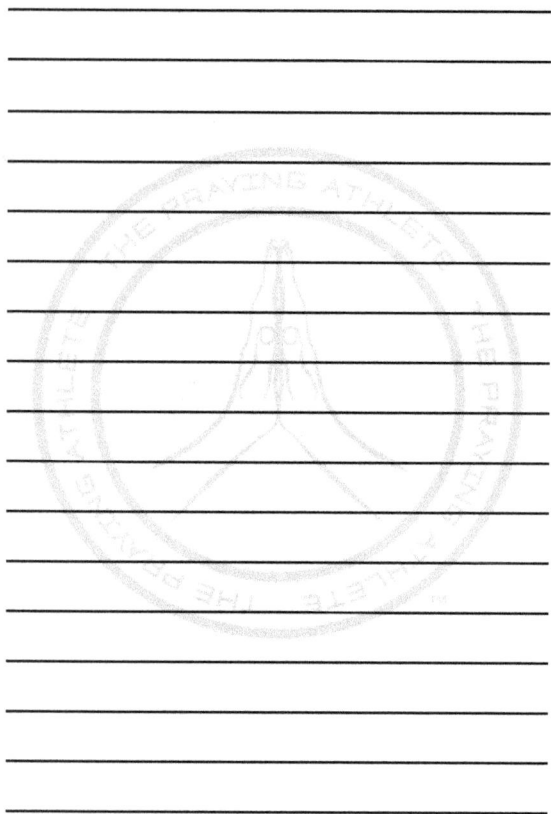

_____

_____

_____

_____

_____

_____

_____

_____

_____

_____

_____

_____

_____

_____

_____

_____

_____

_____

_____

_____

_____

_____

_____

_____

_____

_____

_____

_____

_____

_____

_____

_____

_____

_____

_____

MY QUOTES

_____

_____

_____

_____

_____

_____

_____

_____

_____

_____

_____

_____

_____

_____

_____

_____

_____

_____

_____

_____

_____

_____

_____

_____

_____

_____

_____

_____

_____

_____

_____

_____

_____

ACKNOWLEDGEMENTS

I want to acknowledge and say thank you to all those that
helped with this project:

Nadia Guy
Ashlyn Helms
My Mom & Dad

All of my NFL Clients, current and former, that have
encouraged me to share these words with others.

ABOUT
TPA

The Praying Athlete is a movement that creates an organic culture of prayer through an uplifting community and authentic conversation.

For more information, visit our website **www.theprayingathlete.com**.

Follow us on social media.

 @ThePrayingAthlete

 @Praying_Athlete

 @ThePrayingAthlete

COLLECT ALL
8 VOL.

Our first volume of *The Praying Athlete Quote Book* addresses the topic of playing the game. Quotes and thoughts from Robert B. Walker, paired with Scripture from God's Word, allow readers to get a good idea about what playing a good game looks like.

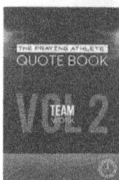

Our second volume of *The Praying Athlete Quote Book* addresses the topic of teamwork. Quotes and thoughts from Robert B. Walker, paired with Scripture from God's Word, allow readers to understand what it means to be a good teammate and surround yourself with people who lift you up.

Our third volume of *The Praying Athlete Quote Book* addresses the topic of growth & preparation for the future. Quotes and thoughts from Robert B. Walker, paired with Scripture from God's Word, allow readers to know that even though the future is uncertain, there is a plan and purpose for everyone.

Our fourth volume of *The Praying Athlete Quote Book* addresses the topic of keeping the right mentality. Quotes and thoughts from Robert B. Walker allow readers to understand how staying in the right mindset can improve overall performance.

Our fifth volume of *The Praying Athlete Quote Book* addresses the topic of staying motivated. Quotes and thoughts from Robert B. Walker allow readers to become motivated to accomplish their goals, even when they feel they are not up to the task.

Our sixth volume of *The Praying Athlete Quote Book* addresses the topic of personal accountability. Quotes and thoughts from Robert B. Walker allow readers to think about how they can better themselves. Whether its ending a bad habit or saying no to anything that may hurt themselves or others, staying accountable will benefit one's character and performance.

Our seventh volume of *The Praying Athlete Quote Book* addresses the topic of living life. This volume is the first part in a two part living life series. Quotes and thoughts from Robert B. Walker give readers a better understanding of how to live life to the fullest.

Our eighth volume of *The Praying Athlete Quote Book* addresses the topic of living life. This volume is the second part in a two part living life series. Quotes and thoughts from Robert B. Walker give readers a better understanding of how to live life to the fullest.

CHECK OUT OUR

THE PRAYING ATHLETE™
PHOTOGRAPHY
QUOTE BOOKS

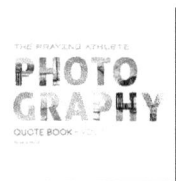

VOL. 1

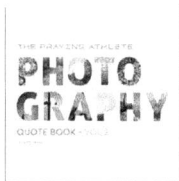

VOL. 2

VOL. 3

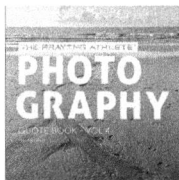

VOL. 4

*The Praying Athlete Photography Quote Book*s celebrate God's glory and magnificence through His creation. They contain photos taken by Robert B. Walker, paired with his words of wisdom, motivation, and inspiration.

www.ingramcontent.com/pod-product-compliance
Lightning Source LLC
Chambersburg PA
CBHW071746020426
42331CB00008B/2194